Sanctuary

PRAYERS FROM THE GARDEN

Sanctuary
PRAYERS FROM THE GARDEN

J. WAYNE PRATT

Printed in the United States of America

Packaged by Pleasant Word, a division of WinePress Publishing, PO Box 428, Enumclaw, WA 98022. The views expressed or implied in this work do not necessarily reflect those of Pleasant Word, a division of WinePress Publishing. Ultimate design, content, and editorial accuracy of this work are the responsibilities of the author.

ISBN 1-4141-0056-6
Library of Congress Catalog Card Number: 2003113368

for Becky:
a precious flower among the many thorns
    that invade the gardens of our memories . . .
a precious flower that grows from
    within the garden of my soul . . .
colorful, delicate and sweetly aromatic;
    she, too, creates an environment of sanctuary
        with the gift of her caring love . . . .

Author's Note

Spending time in the garden, either working with my hands or simply relaxing, has been a cherished time, because it seems to bring me into a closer relationship with Christ. It is a precious time when my mind is cleared, little or no distractions are present, and I am able to hear God's voice speaking to my soul. These prayers emanated from thoughts encountered while tending my garden. And so, the garden has become a place of sanctuary for me.

Thomas Moore, in his encouraging text, *The Re-enchantment of Everyday Life*, speaks about the soul's need for enchantment:

. . . To make local nature a concrete element in daily life is a necessary initial step in the re-enchantment of our individual lives. . . . Enchantment is to a large extent founded in the spirituality inherent in earthly nature. . . . Our task is to re-expand our very idea of spirituality to include the lowliest of things and the most particular and familiar haunts of nature.

In a sanctuary garden one can find not only peace and solitude, but a more important, more exciting sense of re-enchantment for the soul.

—J. Wayne Pratt
Paradise Valley, PA
April, 2003

Contents

SANCTUARY

Creator God,
I've come to cherish this garden as my sanctuary,
  for the intrusions of time and space and hectic schedules
    seem to silently slip away unnoticed.
  Burdens and doubt and confusion
    melt like ice on a warm spring morning
      as the first flowers push their heads heavenward.
  I am alone here, Lord, by myself—
    yet your presence is felt so close at hand.
      My heart is quiet,
        my soul is hushed—so tranquil.
      Peace—your calming peace is present
        and I am able to hear your gentle voice
          speak so clearly and comforting.
  Sometimes ever so gentle and quiet your voice calls
    like the tender song of a bird,
      gently nudging me to ponder a simple thought
        or perform some simple task.
      At other times it is like the haunting shriek
        of a majestic eagle
          disturbing me into needed action,
          or a shocking awareness of my spiritual needs—
            or the needs of others—
              tasks that must be accomplished for you.
    Here, in this garden,
      my sanctuary,
        I find your presence, your calming peace.
    Be with me, O God, as I nurture this garden,
      just as you nurture my soul, my spirit.

Allow me to create in it something which reflects
the beauty you have shared with me.
Thank you, Lord, for this place, this time, this opportunity.

Spring

Spring Thaw

How silent is this garden, my sanctuary.
   The air is still so cold and chilling—yet,
      while the snows begin to melt,
         new life begins to emerge.
   The crocus is pushing its head through the snow—
      toward the heavens,
         announcing this time of renewal.
      Tiny buds appear on the dogwoods and holly.

How the garden reflects the life of Christ,
   buried for a time in the cold, sterile tomb
      and then there is resurrection—new life.
   Your death, O God, bursts forth anew,
      richer, more colorful, more abundant.

Sanctuary: Prayers from the Garden

Lord, in this silence
    and time of dreaming,
        allow my thoughts to focus on transformation
            and new life.
    Help me to feel your resurrection presence as I await
        the dawning of a new season in my journey.

MYSTERY

Bare trees have silently donned their canopies of green—
   shrubs beginning to unfold their emerald leaves,
      the pines and hemlocks add a delightful texture,
      the budding flowers offer color and aroma—
   it's all such a mystery how your touch creates anew
     even after a dark, silent winter
       when all seemed lost, gone forever.
Thank you, God, for putting me in touch with this place
   where I can feel your presence, sense your Spirit,
     and know that you are the God of new and everlasting life.

TRANSFORMATION

This word I've heard so much of lately, Lord—
    at meetings, in discussions, in workshop announcements.
        I've preached the message of transformation to my congregations
            and finally it is genuinely being defined for me
                as I look upon this sacred space and behold
                    your touch upon this garden.
    From seeds, and bulbs, cuttings that I've bought,
        that I've traded, that I've made—
            come plants of strength and beauty
                exhibits of your transforming power
                    taking your creation from humble beginnings
                        to objects of true, exciting beauty.
    What is it I ask, O Lord,
        that causes this change—this transformation
            not only in the garden, but in my life?
                Is it the amount of sunlight, the temperature,
                    the melting snow giving moisture?
                        Is it simply the change of seasons?
    In my own life, I sense it to be the light of your Son, O God,
        your Son who provides warmth to my being,
            the melting of your Spirit into my soul,
                the seasons of my life as I grow and mature in faith.
                    Sometimes this transformation astounds me, Lord,
                        as I anticipate a new season in my journey.

HARMONY

Like a soundless, artistic symphony
   the garden displays an ever unfolding
   quiet masterpiece of melody
      in and out of tune
      with its surroundings.
Yet, there lies within this garden
   a distinct harmony
   pleasant to the eyes and
      a delight to the senses
      for one and all to behold.
A delicate balance of colors
   like the notes of a musical score
   that, taken together, offers a
      continuum of enjoyment
      an enchantment for the soul.
Each tiny flower bud emerging,
   is like a musical note—
   alone—not a complete picture
      but viewed as a garden
      presents a wonderful symphony.
You, O Lord, are the symphony
   of life and all its being
   the artistic masterpiece
      of all creation formed
      a labor of love orchestrated from above.

A PALETTE

In the beginning, Lord, there was something lacking
  it was nothing but a small area of lawn
    lifeless, devoid of any creative touch.
  Bordered by a white picket fence
    it was your offering to me, an empty canvas so to speak
      a creative, genesis story yet to be written.
  Like the artist's palette of gleaming colors
    with patience it became a painting
      this sanctuary garden of ours.
  Slowly and steadily it grew and matured
    revealing more and more each season
      evolving as a splendid composition.
  Each day this garden presents new delights
    new sensations to savor—new experiences to behold
      there is fullness and wonder in this sacred space.
  Times of meditation invoke picturesque images
    of Monet, van Gogh, Renoir
      artists striving to share the beauty of creation.
  But you alone, Lord, are the true and timeless masterpiece
    for in and through you is all of genesis—
      an ever unfolding mystery of creative genius.

Spiritual Oasis

An oasis of comfort and consolation
  which frees me from concerns
    my spirit so open and receptive
      to your embrace, O Lord.
In this sacred vessel of your love
  I find healing, wholeness, and peace
    beyond all hope or measure
      a gift of love that knows no end.
Encircled by a vibrant display
  of trees and shrubs and flowers
    I find comfort, Lord,
      shelter from so many distractions.
Calm, serene, at peace
  in your gentle presence, Lord,
    I find direction for my life
      and nourishment for my soul.
In times of distress and confusion
  my retreat to this sacred sanctuary
    brings renewal and harmony
      peace, sweet peace, of mind.
New hope and happiness emerges
  with each precious flower blooming
    for in their beauty, in their luster
      I discover abundant and eternal life.

BIRDS AND BEES AND BUTTERFLIES

"I come to the garden alone," are the words that fill my mind
  as I sit and dream and meditate on God's Word in my life.
Soon, I am no longer alone, but find I share this sacred space
  with other precious residents of God's creation.
Enter the birds and bees and butterflies
  the most beautiful of God's animals.
They come to drink of the nectar of life
  from that which offers them a meal to feast upon.
Sustenance provided by the blossoms of invitation
  that open their cups of communion for feasting.
Fill my cup, Lord, that in my being, in my living,
  I may be a vessel of communion for others.
Let me, too, Lord, find salvation in your cup of blessing
  and partake of your sweet nectar of life.

A Cup of Coffee

Lord, it's so very quiet and still, so very early.
So soon the sky will be dawning
   to break open yet another glorious day.
So very quiet it arrives—at first—
   and then it just seems to roar down the pike
   with the rising of the eastern sun.
The quiet solitude is shattered by the clamor of the day.
Soon the morning peace will give way to all the demands
   and distractions that come my way.
For the moment, Lord, I bask in the peace—in the solitude—
   firmly grasping my first cup of coffee like a precious jewel.
Time slips ever so slowly by—for now—
   as I dwell amongst the flowers which lift their heads
      to the morning light and the refreshment to come.
I feel your delicate presence, Lord, as I experience the calm
   of this morning and the gentle warmth of your arms
      which surround me and grasp me too.
As I slowly sip my coffee, and gaze upon the flowers,
I think of you, Lord, and all that makes you what you are.
I feel a wonderful sense of joy and peace, kindness, gentleness
   and the warmth of your embrace upon my life.
As this day inches on, may I, too, be gentle and warm and kind;
   a reflection of your character
      a vessel of your cherished gifts.

RENEWAL

The buds begin to flourish
  as if waking from their sleep
    a time of renewal
      a time of rebirth
        from slumber deep and dark.
A miracle of your touch, my Lord,
  that awakens the soul to sing
    proclaiming a glory beyond compare
      all praise to you my Savior
        for the embrace of your breaking dawn.
From that which seems so lifeless
  comes a gem, a jewel to behold
    as you unfold the blossoms
      and grace this garden treasure
        the outgrowth of your love.
A resurrection faith is born
  birthed from heaven on high
    given as a precious gift
      that flowers through the seasons
        and blesses with a beauty rare.
Creation, as I understand it
  is a daily adventure of renewal
    an experience to encounter
      the risen Christ, the Savior
        the One who nurtures me.

A SCARLET SKY

Daylight begins to fade in the western sky and
  a scarlet hue appears like a brilliant watercolor
    painted by you, O God, to awaken our senses.
  How beautiful, how majestic, how reflective
    of the intricacies of the brushstrokes of creation
      and the glory of the heavens.
    This proclamation, Lord, speaks to me in a very powerful way
      reminding me of the beauty of yet another day to dawn
        a day to once again bask in the sunlight of your art.
    Each day, Lord, begins like a painter's fresh canvas
      receptive to your visions and concepts
        ready to be stroked from the artist's palette.
Paint our days with the colors of your choosing, Lord,
    that we, too, might be a canvas of new beginnings
      and beautiful, lasting impressions.

RETREAT

Overwhelmed by the grind of daily life
  so very much on my plate to accomplish—
    I retreat to the garden for renewal
      an emptying of the mind
        my heart's desire made full.
Time and stress slip away in this sacred space, dear Lord,
  and I am thankful for calming rest and spiritual rejuvenation
    that comes even in tiny doses
      and cleanses my inner being
        leaving me to meet the challenges ahead.

QUESTIONS

In this place of calm and comfort, Lord,
dreams so very often come my way
and I think how too frequently
my thoughts and dreams
have come true
only because they were so small.
Have I lost a thirst for life?
Have I been too pleased with self?
Have I been too easily satisfied?
Disturb me, O God, to dream
of broad, new horizons
and greater challenges
to venture into the unknown
in service to your glory
with courage, hope, and strength.
Let me be your hands and feet, O God,
as I strive to carry your message
of grace and hope and peace
to all who would embark
and journey in faith.

MEMORIES

Memories, sweet memories,
flood my very being, O God,
and I experience
a sense of overwhelming joy
in returning to gardens past
sweet savory dreams emerge
transporting me through
time and space and heartache
to gardens experienced
both near and far
romantic places,
relaxing places,
restful places,
where I have always felt your presence
a deep and stirring presence, Lord,
that led me toward your light
and where, eventually,
I was captivated
by a restless stirring
that would not let me go
until I surrendered fully
and gave myself to you.

A Voice in the Wilderness

There is a voice in the wilderness, soft and gentle
   that calls to me in the wilderness of my life, and says,
      "Come, come, my child, to a place of sanctuary
         a garden where your spirit may be renewed."

I journey through my mind
   to a place of rest and contentment
      a place where, yes, my soul will be replenished
         by the life-giving Spirit of God.

Here, in this garden of your creation, Lord,
   my ailing spirit is healed
      restored, refreshed, renewed
         by the One who offers grace, peace, and hope.

SPRING BREEZE

So very gentle, Lord, I feel a delicate breeze
   calming and refreshing to my soul.
As the day journeys on
   a solemn stillness permeates the air
and then, so suddenly, I feel cleansed
   as I lounge in this place of refuge.
   I discover the garden to be not only a haven—
      a sanctuary—a quiet place of rest.
   It has become for me a divine place of healing
      of body, mind, and spirit
   as a refreshing breeze sweeps away
      all cares, concerns, and worries.
      Your Holy Spirit, too, Lord,
         blows about so freely, unrestrained.
      As the breezes blow about this garden
         may your Spirit sweep across my life
      that I may always be refreshed, renewed
         for service in your precious name.

Gethsemane

There is a garden, Lord, that speaks of your unswerving devotion
    to God's will—
        a garden in Gethsemane;
        a garden where you arrived grieved and agitated
            in the springtime of the year
        a garden where you found sanctuary and retreat
            before that awful day that we call "Good."
Here you sought solace and comfort—
    a time to spend in dialog with God.
        So much on your mind
            a hostile world around you
            disciples who fell asleep
            a bitter cup to taste.
Here, you poured out your heart to God asking,
    "if it were possible, let this cup pass from me"
        but in your prefect devotion; in absolute obedience added,
            "yet not what I want but what you want."
Three times you returned to pray
    after finding the disciples sleeping—
        three times you felt abandoned
        and eventually came your rebuke:
    "Are you still sleeping and taking your rest? See,
        the hour is at hand, and the Son of Man is betrayed
        into the hands of sinners. Get up, and let us be going.
        See, my betrayer is at hand."
And from this most sacred garden
    the journey continues on—betrayal, arrest, crucifixion—
    yet, good news follows you as we learn of the greatest gift,
    RESURRECTION!

Summer

SUMMER BRILLIANCE

Summer is finally here, Lord, and
  as I tend to this garden Becky brings me
  a cold glass of lemonade—to quench my thirst.
    I'm reminded not only of my thirst for you
      but how this garden also needs refreshment.
We sit, together, and contemplate our surroundings.
  Grateful for the brilliance of the flowers at their peak—
    masses of color like a beautiful tapestry
      depicting the blaze of creation
        a landscape afire with beauty.
Lord, it gives me joy to offer nurture to this my sanctuary
  just as you nurture me with your Spirit.
I see the flowers grow and burst forth with a sensuous beauty
  that comes from your gentle touch
    and the care I can offer.

Sanctuary: Prayers from the Garden

Thank you, God, that I may care, and—
Thank you, God, for those who care for me.

RAINBOW

Lord, here I am once again,
   tending the garden,
      nurturing it with a gentle touch—

Sunshine penetrates the morning dew,
   violet,
     indigo,
       blue,
         green,
           yellow,
             orange,
             red—
     colors so alive and vibrant—bursting forth
      like a great rainbow from the heavens.
A rainbow that reminds me of God's covenant—
   sealed with the gift of a rainbow
     the God of my life,
       my soul,
         my very being.
Lord, make me ablaze with the colors of this landscape
   flowing from the Creator's hand.
     A garden awash with the love of God's gentle touch
      shining through the darkest of days.

WEEDS

Day after day, Lord, I toil at this garden
    striving to make it a place of beauty—
        a reflection of your touch upon creation.
    Yet, so many weeds continue to invade this sacred space
        and detract from all its grandeur.
    As I see and count the weeds which intrude here
        and produce something of a nuisance
        I am reminded—in a bittersweet way—
            of the multitude of sins which invades your kingdom
            and creates another offensive perspective.
    Lord, as I dig and hoe and work at creating something pure—
        hoping against hope for something of beauty, of purity,
            I realize that it takes so much patience, so much nurture,
                so much love and forgiveness.
        So, too, it must be with you.

You have created something pure, something beautiful
    and yet our sin emerges in so many ways.
    Even with all the patience you possess,
        the nurture you provide, the love you shower upon us,
            and the forgiveness you extend, our sin goes on and on.
    Help us, O God, help me, to live as a disciple of beauty—
        rather than a weed of destruction.
    Help me, through your grace, to flourish in your kingdom
        as an instrument by which others see your beauty,
            your love and forgiveness.

CLAY POT

At the garden's sinuous edge
stands a single terra cotta pot
   a vessel crafted on the wheel
   by the potter's creative hand.
   Simple, earthy and unadorned
   it beckons me to focus my thoughts
      on God—the Master Potter
      on the One who created me.
      Within this simple earthen vessel
      grows a cluster of ornamental grass
         blood-red slender strands
         swaying gracefully in the breeze.
         The blood-red strands assault
         my senses, my very being
            as I am reminded of your Son
            whose blood was shed for me.
            Christ Jesus, too, an earthly vessel
            crafted by the Father's loving hand
               a vessel of love and grace
               a life poured out in sweet surrender.

A Sweltering Day

The days are long and so very hot.
  Summer days can take their toll—
    plants, too, wilt and die if uncared for.
I give thanks, O God, that you care for me;
  that you provide needed refreshment
    and nourishment for my life.
  In the heat of the day my life seems to wilt
    as I reach heavenward for your touch—
      and realize my roots are firmly planted.
  I've heard you referred to as the Master Gardener—
    and now understand how true this saying is—
      that you create so much from so little.
    From humble beginnings, a tiny seed, you nurture and care
      removing impurities, providing refreshment,
        making new from old,
          good from bad,
            strength from weakness,
              beauty from that which is unattractive
                life from that which wilts.
  Thank you, God, for that miracle.

SUNFLOWER

A lonely giant in this garden
  a sunflower so large and bright
    stands tall among the blossoms
      reaching toward the light
        seeking out the heavens
          searching for its creator.
Roots so firmly fixed
  in the fertile ground below
    digging ever so deep
      for the nourishment you give
        holding fast in storm and wind
        a gift of strength you give.
Its mammoth head like a peering eye
  fringed with golden rays
    soulful, seeking, searching
      in the light of a noon-day sun
        a piercing, twinkling luster
          reflecting its tranquil grandeur.
May I, too, Lord,
  stand tall in your creation
    as a witness to your Spirit
      a guidepost for others
        in their search for meaning
          let me point them to the light.

WATERCOLORS

Like an artist's palette splashed with color—
  this garden retreat is vibrant and animated
   with a rainbow of hues that spark the imagination
White so pure like Christ's unyielding grace
  Yellow like the sun so bright
   Orange of the evening light
    Green is the color of the grass God made
     Red is the precious wine of his blood
      Purple tells of a bitter sorrow while
       Pink, so bright, reveals a new tomorrow
So many colors to delight the soul
  So many colors to make it whole
   Vibrant, muted, dynamic and alive
  Your palette of creation, O God,
   beholds the eye and graces the senses
    with such awesome delight.
   You grace my sanctuary, my world, O God,
    and I delight in your presence—
     and rejoice in your creation.

CLOUDS

Evening is drawing near, dinner is over, dishes are washed,
and I tend to some chores in the garden—
a bit of weeding and clean-up to end the day.
As I labor, Lord, peacefully—slowly without haste
clouds above begin to roll in and blanket the sky
deep, dense clouds like soft, colossal pillows above.
How strong and majestic they appear
stampeding across the evening sky so swiftly
as if on a collision course with one another.
Suddenly, at once, the sky turns dark and foreboding
a sign that storms are finding their way to the garden
and will soon burst open with drenching rains.
Deep clouds, dark clouds, clouds of warning
a reminder that God's power is so very awesome
a reminder that God is in control.

SONG OF SOLOMON

Peaceful and so relaxed am I, Lord,
   as I sit surrounded by a feeling of sanctuary—
      reading from Scripture—Song of Solomon—today.
In this garden grows a lovely shrub—a Rose of Sharon
   is its name—graceful and filled with beauty
      it stands as a fair and lovely one.
   Soon, my beloved arrives and I am startled
      startled by her beauty—a lily among the brambles—
       a gesture of serene delight as I see her embraced by the sun.
   The flowers pale beside her—
      her fragrance more pleasing than wine
        richer than myrrh—deeper than a cluster of henna.
A precious gift, like this garden, Lord,
   to one who is so thankful—
      her love beckons and awakens me to rejoice.
She, too, is a delightful garden
   rich in beauty, a mirror of your creation,
      and offers me sanctuary and peace.
Lord, how I rejoice and give thanks—

THE WHITE GARDEN

Meditating as I sit here relaxed, all is at ease
   and I catch myself dreaming—
      dreaming of a pure white garden.
All is white and seemingly so pristine,
   so untouched and heavenly.
Each and every flower,
   each and every shrub,
      bursts forth with blooms of pure white grandeur;
         tulips,
            daffodils,
               roses,
                  lily of the valley,
                     dogwoods and birches,
                        hostas,
                           chrysanthemum,
                              clematis,
                                 lilies, iris—and more.
      There's a fragrance beyond measure
         indescribable and cleansing; so refreshing.
Perhaps a hidden meaning lies behind the vision—
   am I seeing the pure, cloud-like atmosphere
      of that beyond this earthly garden?
Lord, your presence and this dream is so relaxing,
   so very comforting. Pure and spotless heaven must be;
      a garden—a sanctuary to behold.

UNFOLD YOUR LOVE

Unfold your love, O God,
  wrap me in the arms of your embrace.
Unfold your grace, O God,
  encircle me in the folds of your care.
Unfold your mercy, O God
  pour out your lasting forgiveness.
Unfold your truth, O God,
  share new visions of understanding.
Unfold your hope, O God,
  that dreams become realities.
Unfold your light, O God,
  and brighten this pilgrim's path.
Unfold your justice, O God,
  as a means of transformation.
In this lovely creation, my sanctuary
  let me feel the pulse of new birth
through the unfolding of your blessings
  miracles of your promise and giving.

JEWELS

Delicate little jewels they appear to be
tender and frail in the evening light
    but with another look, a closer scrutiny
    an unmatched strength is revealed.
Strength only God's nurture provides
strength to endure the storms of life
    firmly rooted in life-sustaining soil
    grounded in that which provide fortifies.
Perhaps a facade or just a veneer
but hidden inside, deep below the surface
    of the flower so lovely and fair
    lies a God-given framework so strong.
Noble and grand are these delicate jewels
proud, yet not arrogant
    humble and modest they capture your senses
    to delight with an ecstasy rare.
So many jewels in your kingdom, Lord,
all precious beyond measure
    each one sacred to you and
    each one clothed in a beauty beyond compare.

TWILIGHT

My soul, O Lord, thrills at the beauty of this majestic sunset
  as the sun begins to fade, falling so slowly in the western sky.
Bathed in a landscape of God's creation I contemplate
  the clean, clear streams
    the colorful fields, meadows and orchards,
      the green and growing forests
        and the wonder of it all is beyond measure.
How your voice speaks to me in the stillness of twilight—
  the pressures of the day have vanished
    a wondrous sense of calm emerges in my spirit
      as I relax my body, my spirit, myself
        and find myself open to your voice.
I sense the gentle nudge of your leading
  calling me to move my thoughts
    to focus on your calling in my life
      calling me from the briars and brambles of the world
        to the sanctuary of your grace.
Move me, my Lord, I pray, in this twilight time
  to a oneness with your Spirit
    that I may be refreshed for a new day—
      a day of challenges and opportunities
        a day of new beginnings.

MAJESTY

The praise chorus reminds us to: ". . . worship his majesty . . ."
and for me what better place than in the garden—
    a sacred space adorned with the majesty of God's creative gifts
    a sacred space where I can focus on praising my God
        for here I dwell in comfort, in peace
        my praises are pure and undisturbed
            as my thoughts are focused and clear
            and my song of praise is rising to the heavens.
Hear my praise, O God, as it journeys
in a steady, upward path to your throne
    to be gathered together with the offerings of many—
    joined in exaltation to your power and glory
        in thanks for grace and forgiveness freely offered
        in gratitude for countless blessings given
            to you, my Lord, be all praise given
            to you, my God, be all majesty, forever.

DROUGHT

The summer has been so very hot and dry, Lord,
    a drought is what we have been facing—
        some say it is quite serious, a cause for concern.
    It truly amazes me, my God,
        how life is so much like the cycles of nature—
            sometimes dry and parched, sometimes abundant and full.
        There are those times I feel so dry and lifeless
            and like the weather that changes with the wind
                my life changes with the breath of your Spirit.
        The garden, once scorched and crying out for quenching rains
            is finally blessed with the rains of your hand
                and a rebirth is witnessed in its growth.
    I, too, when life leaves me parched and thirsty
        am blessed with a refreshment beyond compare
            a renewing of my soul that infuses new life.
Your Spirit, O God, is the refreshment I need, we all need
    to grow in grace and abundant life—
        to blossom fully as one of your beautiful creations

MOONLIGHT

Sitting quiet in the moonlight
  basking in its translucent glow
    the garden takes on new meaning
      it's a jewel-like effervescent show.
Lord, come, be at my side
  give more meaning to this time
    share with me your presence
      and solace may I find.
Tiny flowers which cast their glow
  are much like precious little jewels
    a necklace wraps this sacred place
      their radiance like a royal crown.
The silence is a treasure
  when life comes crashing in
    asylum, sweet peace now abounds
      your presence felt so near.
In the moonlight comes retreat
  a sense of peace so very dear
    no distractions, no intrusions,
      only calm, soft tranquility.

THE BENCH

Within the framework of the sanctuary garden
    sits a noble granite bench—receptive and inviting
        it is our bench—for the moment anyway.
    Becky and I pause here, quiet, peaceful, contented
        in a dream world—so lush and tranquil
            our cares have gently slipped away—unnoticed.
    Holding hands, the mood is electric
        knowing that without a word being spoken
            the message of love is transmitted.
    Not only our love for each other, Lord,
        but especially our love for you and
            how you brought us together—for a purpose.
    Here we sit and dream of a future
        blessed by your generous gifts
            sharing and caring together—forever.
    Together—we minister in your name
        partners in life and in service—
            mirrors of a heavenly love extended.

SPIRITUAL ENERGY

So simple, so very complex,
　filled with raw emotion,
　　a coalescence of spiritual energy
　　　has been set in motion
　　　　with the creation and nurture
　　　　　of this sacred enclosure.
The garden provides a sense of balance
　between worldly cares and burdens
　　and the need for the spiritual
　　　the need to cultivate a vision
　　　　of timeless communion
　　　　　in a haven of sacred connection.
Contemplation, Lord, brings us together
　the connection like a healing balm
　　happiness replaces frustration
　　　energy replaces fatigue
　　　　refreshment brings regeneration
　　　　my soul, O Lord, is energized.

PRAISE

A warm summer evening finds me sitting in the garden
    chores have been completed, the garden watered and fed—
        It's so relaxing as the day begins to fade
            and the moonlight begins to wash the sky.
    Looking here and there and everywhere in this sacred space
        I can't help but praise you, my God, for your bounty—
            this garden is an explosion of color and texture and aroma
                and I sit here wrapped in your Spirit.
    As I view the flowers around me they, too,
        appear to be offering praise to you, Creator God—
            tulips, daffodils, and lilies voice their praise
                as their blooms stretch heavenward.
        Trees and shrubs, too, look to you, offering their praise
            as blossoms sparkle in the moonlight—
                reflecting a love received and shared
                    for others to witness.
        I thank you, Lord, and offer my praise and gratitude
            that I am called, chosen, so to speak—
                to tend this your creation; this sacred space
                    as a reflection of your love given.

Autumn

CHANGES

Autumn seems to change things, Lord—
  changes that make me think about an ending coming;
    changes that I'm not anxious to witness;
      changes that leave one unsure of the future;
       changes that announce a finality.
  Yet, Lord, change is so very necessary it would seem.
   To move and grow and expand our capabilities
    means to experience change—
      change for the good,
       change which will be of benefit to more than just me.
  Autumn, like old age, is haunting to my soul, Lord.
   Following times of blossom and growth,
    there comes an eerie stillness
      when life seems to be draining away—
       trickling off into the loam of your creation.
   Yet, beyond the eerie stillness,

beyond the lifeblood's draining,
    beyond the sunset of this autumn time of life—
  There awaits a cold and dreary winter season—
    but even further beyond, a springtime of hope and new birth.

CHALICE

This garden, small as it may be, is filled to the very brim
  with the color and texture and aroma of God's creation—and
    as I meditate this morning, deep in thought and prayer,
      the chalice of Christ's last supper is the image in my mind
        a chalice also filled to the very brim with your love, O God..
It is the chalice of forgiveness, the cup of Christ's salvation
  a chalice, once empty, now filled to overflowing
    with the poured out love of Christ Jesus, my Savior.
  Lord, how I truly wish that I might be a chalice also—
    filled with your love, and ready to nourish others
      with the cup of your blessings.
    Fill me, O Christ, fill me to the very brim!

LABYRINTH

Around and around the labyrinth winds
  each turn filled with mystery and reverence
  its path leading to a pivotal center—paradise—
    a center filled with such power and strength;
     a center that gives sanctuary to the soul.
Lead me, O God, through the labyrinth of this garden
  and through the labyrinth of life—to its center—
    to discover wisdom and knowledge;
    to discover strength and encouragement;
    to discover refreshment and purification;
    to discover honest love and caring;
    to discover a new heaven and earth.
Let me walk the paths in each direction, Lord,
  North, South, East, and West—
    so the journey would form a cross
     and then return me to the center
      where I may truly discover the Christ.

HEALING

Feeling down, hurting, worn, world-weary, tired,
  solace and asylum is my present need—
    healing from the captivity of time and tasks—tribulations—
      and so I withdraw to my retreat, my garden, my sanctuary.
In this haven of beauty I meet your Spirit, God,
  and experience your calming presence—
    the pressures of life seem to slip away—unnoticed—
      a relationship is renewed; a relationship that brings peace.
A sense of communion with the Creator, the Healer
  a loving God who offers the sanctuary of serenity—
    a journey to the center of God's shalom—inner peace—
      where renewal and re-creation take place.
Hope, reverence, awe, tranquility
  are renewed and revitalized by encountering the One
    who offers the opportunity of being—instead of doing—
      soul building in a haven of healing.

COBWEBS

Relaxed and peaceful, Lord, I move about this garden
  my eyes filled with the beauty of your creative gifts.
A coating of morning dew blankets the surface and
  offers a sparkling vision of the garden.
As my eyes wander I notice what seems an intrusion
  a trespasser has entered and left its mark.
A cobweb, at first distasteful and annoying—
  but as I stare at its delicate geometry
  sparkling with dew in the autumn morning sun
    I am immersed in its beauty, your creation, O God.
How perfect is the composition—
  did it take hours or days or weeks to complete?
Soft, silken threads interwoven in a complex creative design
  that reflects an engineering miracle beyond compare.
At first repulsed by this intrusion, I now delight in its presence
  and find myself gazing intently at the wonder displayed.
Its purpose confuses—something crafted in such beauty
  to secure another meal—a captive to be devoured.
Lord, is it possible that such beauty is really a trap?
  Is that how we are enticed and devoured by the world?
Lord, let me see inner beauty as a captivating force—
  let me move to appreciate what's inside of myself—
    inside of others—inside of everything
      as the catalyst of your grace and righteousness.

THE PATH

The path to this sacred garden
  the path that allows entry
  the path built in faith
    winds across a wilderness
    a wilderness, or so it seems,
      compared to the beauty of the destination.
As long days pass into darkness
  and then as morning—a new day—is revealed
  I find the path much like life on earth
    turning and twisting, with new surprises to behold
    surprises around each and every bend in the road
      experiences that both delight and confuse.
As I grow and mature in my faith, Lord,
  the path seems much straighter, my focus clearer
  the wilderness not so harsh—
    a smoother transition in life
    as my journey continues
      and awakens me to new vistas and horizons.
I delight, Lord, in knowing that the path of life
  my journey in faith and discernment
  leads to a truly sacred moment in time and space
    a place where love abounds and peace is truly present
    and that the destination reveals your truths
      your promises, and your presence.

DANCE

A gentle breeze wisps through the garden
  as your breath flows beneath the trees
    and delicate, tender flowers seem to sway
      in a dance to stir the soul.
You, too, have danced, my Lord,
  in times of joy and pain
    a holy dance, a sacred dance,
      a dance that never ends.
The dance of celestial creation
  when the world was begun
    a holy dance of genesis
      when you choreographed this earth.
A dance of Sabbath healing
  when some turned away
    and would not follow
      but, yes, the dance goes on.
There was a day so dark, so lonely,
  no doubt you felt alone
    as the shadows filled the sky
      and, yes, the dance goes on.
Lead me in this dance, O God,
  lead me into the rhythms of life so full
    and I will follow, follow you
      wherever you may dance.

SURRENDER

I surrender to the call of this sanctuary
  an invitation to a time of grace and gentleness
    which ushers in reverence and hope—
      a time when my soul is transformed;
        my spirit empowered.
My inner life and vision, O God,
  are restored and refreshed by your presence
    my creativity, my compassion—
      expanded as paradise welcomes me
        to a feeling of wholeness.
In the garden sanctuary my spiritual needs
  are renewed and revitalized each day
    as I surrender to your call—
      surrender my worldly cares
        to the guardian and garden of my soul.
Here in this sacred place I experience
  a re-enchantment of my daily life
    this garden, Lord, surrounds my body—
      I'm in a state of being rather than doing
      imagining this paradise unfolding.

GRACE

Your grace, O God, is like the gentle rains of spring
    refreshing, renewing, life-giving—
        refreshing in that grace abounds for one and all
            renewing in that my sagging spirit is lifted
                life-giving in that
                    grace can heal wounds,
                    grace can tear down barriers,
                    grace can cleanse and make pure,
                    grace can open closed doors, and
                    grace can guide us on our journey.
Grace I have received, O God, and may grace I offer
    to touch the life of my neighbor, my friend, my foe.
        As I have received, so may I give—
            unselfishly, without hesitation
                as an offering to you, my Lord and Savior
                    the One who heals
                    the One who breaks the chains and barriers
                        that I create in my life
                    the One who has opened so many doors
                        especially the door that leads to service
                    the One who guides me on my journey—
                        a journey that starts in a sacred garden, a sanctuary
                        and leads to Kingdom living.

SOLITUDE

A riveting sense of solitude envelopes me in this sanctuary
and I experience the gentleness of my soul being reenchanted.
There is a rapture and ecstasy here, Lord,
not present in the preoccupations of daily life.
Once again, I feel a childlikeness, an innocence
where I am opening myself to your Spirit.
Lead me, Lord, and awaken my heart to your stirrings
that I may offer solitude to those whose lives I touch.
Here, Lord, you erase my fears and doubts
and in the stillness calm the cravings of my heart,
Challenge me, Lord, as my soul is re-enchanted
to be a soul-mate to those whose lives I touch.
Here, Lord, you offer renewal and refreshment
and I am awakened to new possibilities.
Arouse within in me, Lord,
the ability to empower others in your name.

BEATITUDES

Bless this garden, dear Lord,
   that it may grow and provide sanctuary
    a heavenly retreat for the spirit.
   In times of mourning and sorrow
    allow your presence to fill this place
     offering comfort to those who grieve.
   For those who hunger and thirst
    for virtue and righteousness and purity
     find their yearnings satisfied.
   May this garden reflect your mercy, Lord,
    that all who find respite in its serenity
     be moved to bequeath mercy to others.
   May this garden be a place of peace
    empowering your children to offer harmony
     in their living and in their caring.
   When feeling persecuted, mistreated, abused
    a time in this sanctuary, through your grace,
     will be a reminder that no one suffered like you.
   In all the shadow experiences of life
    when all seems dark and forlorn—no future—
     help me to rejoice, O Lord, for indeed
     the reward will be greater yet.

MUSIC

In the soft and tender silence
there is music to be heard.
Unlike the discord of the world outside
it is a harmony of tranquil inner peace.

Is it my heart beating that I hear
or my soul offering grateful praise?
Such music often seems a stranger
as I journey forth in time, in life.

Set the music playing, Lord,
that I may join the happy chorus
and lift my humble voice to you
in vibrant hope and adoration.

Tune me, Lord, attune me
and keep me in pure harmony
with the score you lay before me
sweet music for the soul.

A Fragrant Incense

Lord, the day has been one of tremendous beauty
  an autumn day rich in color as the
    reds, and oranges,
     yellows and greens
      of the mountainside
       offer a tapestry of wonder.
As I sit here in the garden—deep in contemplation
  I am moved as the winds begin to stir
    and the atmosphere is filled with a delightful aroma
    the sweet incense of burning leaves
     another sign of autumn's arrival
     a change of seasons once again.
The burning leaves create a delightful incense
  an aroma which calls me to worship
    and so, my God, I offer to you my thanks and praise
     for a day given—freely
      a day received—thankfully
       a day with opportunity to worship.
Thank you, God, for changing seasons
  and reminders that you are the Creator.

AUTUMN WINDS

The winds, O God, begin to brew
  and race across my garden
    as if to chase away these pleasant days.
  They rage and howl, displaying their bold indignation
    pushing aside the vibrant colors, textures, and
      delightful aromas of this autumn season.
  Now they gust, Lord, hear them blow
    as they gather in strength and intensity
      sweeping us into dark days ahead.
  These winds of autumn evenings
    seem to dance and whirl and spin
      their tale of a coming transformation.
  As I sit and write, offering my prayers to you, Lord
    the pages of my journal turn in the wind
      blowing away thoughts and meditations.
  Soon the time will come, soon the days will chill,
    and I will no longer be able to seek the warmth,
      and welcome, and comfort of this garden.

DEPRESSION

"Hello darkness, my old friend . . ." chime the words
to that haunting song of my youth so long ago
and now I discover a feeling of safety in moments of darkness.
Trials and tribulations have left me in a state of depression, Lord,
and I wonder how I might climb out of this wilderness
that has captured my being and wrestles my emotions.
Struggles seem to be everywhere—clouding my focus
with a tension that I cannot release or break free from—
they hold on like battle scars to the mind.
Free me, Lord, from this beast that dwells within
offer the blessing of sanctuary, the gift of peace of mind
that I might go forth in the light of your love.
Only by your grace, Lord, can burdens be lifted
tensions eased and obstacles overcome
so a new day will dawn and provide necessary light.
A divine light is needed as I wrestle and struggle with life
so that your mercy, Lord, can unleash this burden
and break this curtain of darkness that surrounds me.
The light now reenters, as a miracle—
my eyes and emotions begin to focus
as burdens are lifted and anguish is resolved.
The curtain of hope and joy parts wide open—
healing is taking place and
wholeness is being reconstructed and I
Thank you, God.

Autumn Leaves

Autumn brings about a drastic alteration to the landscape—
    leaves at first change from green
        to reds and yellows and oranges,
            the hillsides are awash in a blanket of colors
                a dramatic backdrop to my sanctuary, my garden.
But, oh so quickly, Lord,
        the leaves begin their final journey
            as they change to a dreary brown
                and then begin to drop—
                    and fall downward to the ground.
And while this change at first looks lifeless and drab,
        your hand is at work in mysterious ways—
            it is not a blanket of death,
                but a cover of life as these leaves
                    will provide nourishment for tomorrow.
As they decompose and rot away
        the soil is nourished anew
            and in days ahead plant roots will spread
                seeking this life-giving resource
                    needed for new growth; new life.
Thank you, God, for this miracle,
        that from what seems lifeless, drab and dreary,
            life-giving nourishment is provided—
                a strange and mysterious phenomenon
                    that is all a vital part of your creation.
Witnessing this awesome change
        I begin to realize that when I, too, am falling

you are there to provide nourishment for days ahead
as I struggle in my faith journey
reaching out, my roots seeking sustenance.
Thank you, God, for so many miracles.

LAMENT

Autumn winds begin to blow—
  a damp chill permeates the garden
    and a lament begins to fill my heart.
Leaves are dropping ever so quickly
  signaling the coming end of a season
    with winter on its way.
Flower heads begin to drop—
  the seeds disperse and disappear
    as autumn breezes channel them away.
My heart is sad, O Lord, as this season
  seems to take away my joy;
    my sanctuary soon will be but a memory.
But only for a time, a brief moment in your sight
  as days slip quickly by
    it will return again and provide my soul delight.
For now, dear Lord, I must let go
  and commend it to you care
    through cold and silent days ahead.
Bless, O Lord, this sacred space
  may it sleep in your sweet peace—
    and bloom again when seasons change once more.

Winter

SNOWS OF WINTER

It is the wintertime of your creation, Lord,
   and glistening snow blankets this precious garden—
      my retreat, my sanctuary.
I am huddled inside, where it is warm and comfortable.
   Staring out the window
      I dream of what lies ahead—
      I dream of working the soil,
         planting new plants, offering food,
            quenching the thirst of these beds.
Pristine and pure,
   all is now wrapped in the garb of this anxious time.
      It lies not in a cold, silent death
         but rather enjoys a still, peaceful sleep
      awaiting that glorious moment of resurrection.
   That joyous time when you allow life to spring forth anew,

wrapped in all the vibrant colors
and textures
and aromas
that bring meaning to creation.
Thank you for the gift of this sanctuary—
a sacred space in my heart, my mind—
a space where I find your presence so close at hand.
Thank you, God.

SHADOWS

Shadows dance across a blanket of snow
a mystical sight in the moonlight glow
flickering softly on this special night.
A winter garden is deeply mysterious
weaving a web of intricate shadows—
deep, dark lines intertwined on a canvas white.
The shadows dance and jump and play
as I chase them with open eyes
seeking to name patterns that will delight.
Lord, as I watch and wait and hope
for your gift of love, a gift to treasure
it shines now in a beam so bright.
A star shines from heaven above
leading the way—and quickly I realize,
Lord, this is Epiphany—a magi night.

COVENANT

In so many ways, O God,
   this garden is not mine, but yours.
    You call me to be its steward, its keeper—
     a covenantal relationship.
      And so, I must let go; relinquish control
      and embrace a joyful partnership.
       In my letting go, Lord, you draw me closer
       to you and your creation.
        Bind me, Lord, in your covenant of love
        and never let me go.

EDEN'S GARDEN

It was in a garden that the Creation Story began—
   a sacred enclosure we hail as Eden.
   Night and day, waters and dry land,
      plants yielding seed, trees bearing fruit.
      Living creatures of every kind,
         to inhabit the holy garden.
         And God you saw that it was good
            and so created humankind—from the dust of the earth.
You blessed them, Lord, and gave them dominion
   over all of your creation and called them care for it.
   Here, too, a covenant bound the relationship
      yet, soon fractured—never to be the same.
      Banished, exiled, sent forth from the garden
         to toil amongst the serpents.
         A covenant broken, fractured, corrupted,
            in greed and desire it was undone.
O God, your covenants have been made and broken
   from the very beginning; throughout the ages.
   As your children, Lord, make us attentive to the holy Word
      that we may strive to keep the covenant intact.
      Help us see the way to a joyful covenant experience
         and find us, at last, bound by your promises.

STARRY NIGHT

A cold, winter night surrounds me, Lord,
    and I stare at the silence of sanctuary.
Still the trees are bare, casting their shadow
    across the barren landscape of the garden—
        all is hushed, quiet, and still.
    The stars shine brightly on this cold winter evening,
        casting an eerie light upon garden remnants
            lying quiet against the drifts of snow.
My mind, Lord, recalls the colors and textures yet to emerge
    but for now there is a silence
        and I can dream of a creative portrait before me.
    A wonderful picture like Van Gogh's "Starry Night"
        with its swirls of light, hauntingly vibrant
            breaking through the night.
    I hear the words of the singer
        as he tells the story of Vincent, also once a pastor,
            and the creative vision you shared with him.
        How this world wasn't ready
            for something "as beautiful as you," says the song.
Gracious God, even in darkness
    I am reminded of a gentle place of sanctuary
        where my mind and heart captures your presence.
    Even in the still, dark barren landscape of winter
        your presence is here and I feel your starry light.

DREAMING

Sitting at the window on a clear, bright winter night—
  a freshly fallen snow blankets the garden.
The moon is full and casts a mystical light.
 Shadows from the remnants of plants and shrubs
  fall across their white cover—a strange, yet delightful sight.
Seeing the barren grasses, the tiny evergreens, and,
  a multitude of branches
    poking through their cover; a study in contrasts—
      a garden in snow and shadow;
       a garden in black and white.
My excitement builds; my mind wanders.
  Thoughts of new plants being placed here and there
    to fill the gaps and add more interest.
  It causes me to dream, Lord, wondering what lies below;
    what lies ahead. Will springtime ever come?
Lord, patience is a virtue, I know, yet
  the dreams I dream, the visions I see,
    bring hope for a new tomorrow—
  a tomorrow filled with even more beauty—
  a beauty that is a precious gift from you, my God.

DARKNESS

An eerie darkness envelops this night, O God,
  and I anxiously await the dawning light.
As I slip into slumber rest, suspended in time
  my thoughts are centered on the garden
    a garden lying outside my window
      wrapped in a cloak of black and white
        as if pictured in an old time photograph.
Snows of clean, clear white cover the ground, Lord,
  in sharp contrast to the pitch black night
    where remnants of a season past
      are clothed in a dancing, shadowy robe
        like precious jewels displayed on rich, black velvet.
My thoughts find me sitting in the garden
  on a sunny day of long, long ago
    and I realize, Lord, I am dreaming—
      dreaming about a bright and growing future
        not only for my sanctuary but also for my life.
My dream takes me to gardens unknown
  where I am but a stranger, a traveler in the night
    seeking refuge and respite
      from a time of darkness and slumber rest
        to coming seasons of light and life and achievement.
Hear my prayer, O God, for days of light and growth—
  surprise my inner being with blossoms bright and beautiful
    of quenching rains and nourishment given freely
      that I may awake to the fullness of creation
        and true sanctuary is but a step away.

DYING

Lord, the winter this year is taking its toll—
  loss, death, grief surround me in ministry
    first one call, then another from the funeral parlor
      a challenge to my emotions, my inner spirit
        that at times leaves me drained and reaching out.
Sometimes I just don't know how I carry on—
  striving to be a comfort, a shoulder, an uplifting presence
    were it not for your walking with me
      no doubt I fall and falter and fail but,
        thankfully, you offer strength, assurance and guidance.
You grace the weary, O God, the tired, and forlorn
  and answers come from the heavens above
    removing stress and anxiety
      calming the storms that abound in life and ministry
        how precious are you to me, O God, my inner strength.
It is in death, or in losing one's life in faith
  as Scripture reminds us, that life is truly gained
    that life with all its tragedies, trials, and tribulations
      can be lived with a wondrous sense of joy
        as a cross is taken up—in a life given for others.

BLIZZARD

The blinding snow is falling, fast and heavy
  deeper and deeper until the garden disappears.
    The landscape seems lifeless and choked,
      how much more will cover the ground.
Over a foot at last count, no end in sight.
  Everything has disappeared, Lord.
    Will my sanctuary ever return?
    Will it ever be renewed—rediscovered?
  Hallowed is this place, even in bleak mid-winter.
    For the garden, too, needs its rest—
      a time to recoup and build vitality
        for its glorious display in another season.
  In this time of slumber, Lord,
    provide a needed rest—
      create a storehouse of energy
        needed for springtime transformation.
  Empower this sacred garden, Lord,
    for the journey that lies ahead
      that it may be a reflection of your creative touch.

SILENT NIGHT

Silent is the night, my Lord,
  a night most holy and divine
    in the stillness,
      in the silence,
        in the bitter cold,
          I am drawn to the garden
            even if for but a moment.
Something very dear
  something quite precious
    calls me to reflect on this moment
      to experience Incarnation
        in a new and wholesome way.
The miracle of Christmas
  floods my entire being
    as I feel transported
      to a distant place and time
        and I become a witness
          to Christ's nativity.
Thank you, God, for the stillness,
  thank you for the gentle silence
    which allows me the opportunity
      to share in this miracle
        in a new and wholesome way.

A WINTER CHILL

I have ventured out on this winter morning
   hoping to feel your presence, Lord,
      but am first struck by a winter's chill
         that permeates deep inside my being.
Here I stand, in a bare and lonely garden
   dreaming of days gone by
      when warmth filled this paradise
         and your presence felt so close.
Be near me now, O Lord,
   as I struggle with a loneliness
      that hurts deep inside my soul
         and chills my once joyous spirit.
Almost frozen, in a trance like state
   my prayer rises to your throne
      and I feel a glow, a tiny spark
         that re-ignites my passion, my hope.
Like a cold and dreary winter
   this chill within will pass
      and brighter days will soon emerge
         bringing warmth to my spirit.
Thank you, God, for changing seasons
   and changes within the heart and spirit
      that give me great assurance
         of your presence within my soul.

SILENCE

In these dark days of winter, Lord,
    when all seems so very silent
        quiet beyond one's imagination
            you make your presence known
                in such subtle, gentle ways.
The silence can be so very lonely
    for a world that craves excitement
        boredom can overpower
            apathy can easily conquer
                indifference can take hold.
And, yet, despite the lurking stillness
    despite the bitter loneliness
        you are there to comfort and console
            and bring the soul relief.
Thank you, Lord, for walking with me
    in times of doubt and despair
        your love and encouragement
            breaks the dividing walls of silence
                and brings a scene of peace.

TRACKS

In this silent night of winter
  when all is dark and still
    my gaze upon the garden
      brings a sense of growing curiosity
        as I begin to focus on the footprints
          that have left an deep impression
            across the fresh fallen snows
              which blanket the garden's floor.
God's creatures have made a quiet visit
  pausing, probing, exploring all around
    in search of food or shelter
      or perhaps a long, lost friend.
There is comfort in this sanctuary
  the gift of welcome hospitality
    extended as an open door.
  Thank you, Lord,
    for the welcome you provide
      freely offered, freely given
        to all creatures—great and small.

ICICLES

Icicles dangle from their perch on the limbs of many plants
hanging ever so silent in the morning sun
dripping, dripping ever so slow and methodically
as the warmth of this new day brings a change
a change that erases the glistening prisms
that sparkle a light so captivating.
Lord, here I sit breathing the cold, crisp air
and am entranced by the icicles which melt before me
Why, O God, I ask, does something so beautiful
have to turn to nothingness and disappear—
to slowly drip away into oblivion?
Will my life be the same?
Their sparkle, their glitter, as they dance and drip away
will never be truly lost for they are made of mystery
the mystery of your creating hand
remain forever, I plead as they continue
continue to shrink and slowly disappear
stay in my mind, at least, as a memory.
Hang on, O tiny icicle, hang onto that branch
share with me more of the rainbow of colors
as the morning light burns its glow into your being
hang in there, little one, hang on
that I may bask in your light.
Gone—but not forgotten, but a memory now
that turns into dreams of days ahead
when I may once again enjoy your presence
so much like Jesus, gone perhaps, in a way
but always with me—a glistening light.
Thank you, God!

CREATION

In the beginning it was a nothingness
   devoid of any life
      lacking any signal of welcome,
         any sign of hospitality.
      This space was devoid of any creative grace
         looking like a barren desert in winter
            unkempt—lifeless—hostile—
               words that frighten and menace.
         Your breath, your tender touch, O God,
            will breathe new life into this barren land
            and allow a genesis to be seen—
               a new life to be witnessed as
                  the winter of discontent slowly fades away.
         Creating God, embellish me with your presence
            and banish discontent that in this sacred space
               will be fresh life symbolizing your revelation—
               transformation and tranquility—
                  new birth amidst the chaos of a day gone by.

Epilogue

A Thank You Prayer
For all the seasons the garden encounters
  and all the seasons of life—thank you, God.
   Thank you for this sacred space—my sanctuary
     where I can experience you in so many different ways.
     I find you in the colors, in the textures,
       in the sweet and delicious aromas.
     I find you there in all the seasons of the year
       winter, spring, summer and autumn.
     I find you there in sweltering, arid days
       thirsting for you.
     I find you there in the coolness of the evening
       a gentle breeze stirring my soul.
     I find you on those winter days,
       a shadow dancing on the snow.
    I find you in this sacred space—ever-present,
       ever there to guide and nurture me in faith.
Thank you, God, for your presence.
   THANK YOU!

To order additional copies of

Have your credit card ready and call:

1-877-421-READ (7323)

or please visit our web site at
www.pleasantword.com

Also available at: www.amazon.com

CPSIA information can be obtained at www.ICGtesting.com
Printed in the USA
BVOW080538271112

306513BV00001B/99/A